True Survival

WHALESHIP ESSEX

DISASTER AT SEA

Virginia Loh-Hagan

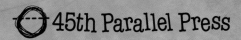

45th Parallel Press

Published in the United States of America by Cherry Lake Publishing
Ann Arbor, Michigan
www.cherrylakepublishing.com

Reading Adviser: Marla Conn MS, Ed., Literacy specialist, Read-Ability, Inc.
Book Designer: Felicia Macheske

Photo Credits: © Willyam Bradberry/Shutterstock.com, cover; © FloridaStock/Shutterstock.com, 5; © EvgeniiAnd/
Shutterstock.com, 6; © LouieLea/Shutterstock.com, 9; © Judy Tejero/Shutterstock.com, 11; © worldswildlifewonders
/Shutterstock.com, 12; © stockelements/Shutterstock.com, 14; © Damsea/Shutterstock.com, 17; © Rich Carey/
Shutterstock.com, 19; © Roman Stetsyk/Shutterstock.com, 20; © Andrey Yurlov/Shutterstock.com, 23; © Chepe
Nicoli/Shutterstock.com, 24; © GagliardiImages/Shutterstock.com, 27; © Charles Curtis/Shutterstock.com, 29

Graphic Elements Throughout: © Gordan/Shutterstock.com; © adike/Shutterstock.com; © Yure/Shutterstock.com

45th Parallel Press is an imprint of Cherry Lake Publishing.

Library of Congress Cataloging-in-Publication Data

Names: Loh-Hagan, Virginia, author.
Title: Whaleship Essex : disaster at sea / by Virginia Loh-Hagan.
Description: Ann Arbor, Michigan : Cherry Lake Publishing, 2017. | Series:
 True survival | Includes bibliographical references and index.
Identifiers: LCCN 2017033514| ISBN 9781534107717 (hardcover) | ISBN
 9781534109698 (pdf) | ISBN 9781534108707 (pbk.) | ISBN 9781534120686
 (hosted ebook)
Subjects: LCSH: Essex (Whaleship) | Shipwrecks—Pacific Ocean. | Shipwreck
 survival—Pacific Ocean.
Classification: LCC G530.E77 L65 2017 | DDC 910.9164/9—dc23
LC record available at https://lccn.loc.gov/2017033514

Cherry Lake Publishing would like to acknowledge the work of The Partnership for 21st Century Skills.
Please visit *www.p21.org* for more information.

Printed in the United States of America
Corporate Graphics

table of contents

chapter one

Whale Hunters

What is the *Essex*? What is whaling? Who was on the ship?

The *Essex* was an American **whaler**. Whalers were special ships. They were used to catch whales. They had **harpoons**. Harpoons are long spears.

The *Essex* was from Nantucket. Nantucket is in Massachusetts. It's a small island. It was the world's whaling capital. It had more than 70 whalers.

The *Essex* was 87 feet (26.5 meters) long. It weighed 239 tons. It was made of white oak. This is strong wood. It had three **masts**. Masts are long poles on ships. They support the sails. The *Essex* had five small boats. Each boat was 28 feet (8.5 m) long.

The *Essex* was a trading ship before it became a whaler.

People hunted whales. This is called **whaling**. People ate whale meat. They used whale oil.

Whaling was hard work. Whalers sailed. They looked for whales. When a whale was spotted, sailors acted. They sent little boats out. There were about six men in a boat. They got close to the whale. They threw harpoons. Harpoons are connected to ropes on the boat. Sailors hitched their boats to the whales. They tired out the whales. Then, they killed the whales. They used **lances**. Lances are long, sharp knives on poles. Sailors towed the dead whale to the whaler. They brought it on board. They cut it apart. They got oil and meat.

◄ Whale oil was used for lamps and lanterns.

spotlight biography

Herman Melville was born in 1819. He died in 1891. He was a writer. He wrote *Moby Dick*. This book is based on the *Essex*. Melville was a teacher. Then he became a sailor. He worked on the whale ship called *Acushnet*. This gave him knowledge about whaling. He heard about a white whale ramming a ship. He met Owen Chase's son. Chase told him about the *Essex*. He gave Melville his father's notes. All this inspired Melville to write *Moby Dick*.

The *Essex* was an old ship. It made a lot of money. People thought it was lucky. It hunted sperm whales.

The *Essex* took a new job. It was going to the South Pacific. The trip would take 2 years and 6 months.

The captain was George Pollard Jr. He was the youngest whaler captain. He was 29. This was his first trip as captain. The first **mate** was Owen Chase. A mate is an officer on a ship. They had worked together before. The second mate was Matthew Joy. Thomas Nickerson was the cabin boy. He was 14. He was the youngest member of the **crew**. Crew are workers. There were 21 people on the ship.

Whales have a lot of blubber. Blubber is fat.

chapter two

Thar She Blows!

How did the trip start out? How did the whale attack the *Essex*?

The *Essex* left Nantucket on August 12, 1819. It sailed for 2 days. It was hit by a big wave. It got knocked to the side. It almost sank. It lost a sail. Some boats got damaged. The crew was scared. Pollard wanted to return to Nantucket. Chase disagreed. Pollard kept going. He led them to an island. He fixed the ship. They set sail again.

Two months later, they saw whales. The sailors hunted. Then, they moved on. They hunted where they could. But there weren't many whales left.

They heard about a new place. It was farther away. Not many whalers went there. So there should be lots of whales. They wanted to go. But they needed more food and supplies.

The *Essex* collected more than 450 barrels of whale oil.

They sailed to an island. They fixed a leak. They caught more than 300 giant tortoises to eat. They caught them alive. They let some roam around the ship.

On November 20, 1819, a **pod** of whales was spotted. Pods are groups. The small boats set out. Sailors went to harpoon the whales. A baby whale hit Chase's boat. The boat got damaged. Chase returned to the *Essex*. He wanted to fix it.

One of the boats got a whale. Then, they lost control. The whale dragged the boat away from the *Essex*. This is called a "Nantucket sleigh ride."

Sailors thought tortoises could live without food or water.

explained by
science

Sperm whales are huge. They have big heads. They have big round bumps on their heads. They have the largest brains. They have teeth. They eat thousands of pounds of food a day. There's no need to be scared of sperm whales. Sperm whales are calm animals. They rarely attack. They attack when they're being attacked. They attack when they mistake humans for other sea animals. They mainly eat giant squid. They swallow squids whole. They have four stomach areas. There's no air inside their stomachs. They have a large throat. This lets them swallow large animals. They could swallow humans. But they don't. They hunt 3,000 feet (914 m) deep. This is too deep for humans.

Nickerson saw a huge white whale. It was as big as the ship. The whale sped toward the ship. It rammed into the ship. It hit the left side. It passed under the ship. It came up for air. It attacked again. It hit the front of the ship. It kept attacking.

The *Essex* **listed**. Listing means tilting. Pollard asked, "My God, Mr. Chase, what is the matter?" Chase said, "We have been **stove** by a whale." Stove means hit. The whale stopped. It swam away. The *Essex* never saw it again.

The ship sank in 2 days.

◄ The sailors were more than 1,500 miles (2,414 km) west of Peru.

chapter three

Stranded at Sea

What happened to the men at sea? What did they do to avoid dying of hunger?

The crew needed to escape. They took what they could. They took 300 pounds (136 kilograms) of biscuits. They took several barrels of water. They took some tortoise meat. They took some guns. They took some sailing tools.

They got into three small boats. Pollard, Chase, and Joy were in charge of each boat. They got away from the sinking ship.

They were far away from land. They were **stranded**. Stranded means stuck.

Pollard wanted to go to one of the Pacific islands. This was 30 days away. Chase disagreed. He was afraid of **cannibals**. Cannibals are people who eat people. Chase and Joy wanted to go to South America. So that's what they did. This was a longer trip.

Pollard wanted to go to Tahiti. Some think everyone would have survived had they gone.

would you?

- **Would you go whaling?** People in Iceland, Norway, and Japan still hunt whales. They kill 1,500 whales a year. Many people think whaling is cruel. They think whales should be protected.

- **Would you sail in the ocean?** Sailing is one of the safest ways to travel. But some people are scared of being on the ocean. There are storms. There are sharks. There are pirates. Pirates steal things from ships.

- **Would you work on a ship?** Working on a ship is hard. You're stuck at sea. You sleep in small spaces. You might get seasick. But you get to feel sea breezes. You get to see sea animals. You get to see new places.

The boats weren't in good shape. They had many leaks.

They landed at Henderson Island. They found a small spring. They ate birds, crabs, eggs, and grass. They ate everything in about a week. They had to leave. But three men chose to stay.

The crew set sail again. They headed to Easter Island. They hit bad weather. Sea animals damaged their boats. Some sailors went crazy. Sailors got sunburned. Sharks circled them at night.

Pollard's crew faced many dangers while at sea.

They were hungry. Most of their food was soaked in seawater. They were thirsty. They drank their own pee. Men began to die. Joy died first. He was sewn into his clothes. He was buried at sea.

They ran out of food. As men died, they kept the dead bodies. They had to eat the bodies. They ate the bodies of seven men. They were desperate.

◄ Sailors had to make hard choices.

chapter four

Saved at Last!

How did they get rescued? Where were they reunited?

The boats got separated. The men didn't have food. They didn't have water. They were stranded for about 90 days. They were near death.

A sailor in Chase's boat saw a ship. It was a British ship. It was called the *Indian*. The crew sailed to it. They were rescued. This happened on February 18, 1820.

Pollard's boat was also saved. They were near the South American coast. The *Dauphin* saved it. It was an American whaler. A sailor saw Pollard's boat. Pollard and his men were confused. They were scared. They didn't know they were being rescued.

The boats got separated because of storms.
Joy's boat was never seen again.

Some believe they found Joy's boat. They found bones of three men.

The *Dauphin* sailors were shocked. One sailor said the *Essex* men were "sucking the bones of their dead **mess mates**." Mess mates are fellow sailors. This happened on February 23, 1820.

All the survivors were taken to Valparaiso. This is a city in Chile. The men healed. They got better. They told their story. They told about the other survivors on Henderson Island.

The *Surrey* was an Australian ship. It went to save the three men. The ship had a hard time getting to Henderson Island. There was a strong tide. But the rescue was a success. This happened on April 9, 1821.

survival tips

TRAPPED ON A SINKING SHIP!

- Know all the exits. Know the stairways.

- Know how to wear a life jacket. Don't wear it until you need to. Life jackets can be bulky. They're hard to move around in.

- Go up to the deck. Don't go to the inner levels of the ship.

- Find the "muster station." This is where people gather in emergencies. Jumping into the water should be the last thing you do.

- Listen for the captain to say, "Abandon ship." Don't jump overboard. Get into lifeboats.

- Connect the lifeboats. Share things with other survivors. Support each other. You have a better chance of being seen and rescued as a big group.

chapter five

Life After the Whale

What did the survivors do? What happened to Pollard? What happened to Chase?

The survivors returned to Nantucket. Chase wrote a book about his survival. Nickerson also wrote his story.

The survivors all went back to sea. Pollard became captain of the *Two Brothers*. This ship was another whaler. It was in a storm. It got wrecked. Pollard joined another ship. That ship got wrecked. Pollard became known as a "**Jonah**." A Jonah is an unlucky sailor. Nobody would hire him to sail. He quit sailing. He became a night watchman. Every year on November 20, he locked himself in his room. He didn't eat. He did this to honor the *Essex*.

The people in whaling towns depended on good luck and good weather.

Rest in Peace

"The captain goes down with the ship." This is a famous saying. Many captains feel responsible for their ships. They don't run away from sinking ships. They save people. Or they'll die trying. Edward J. Smith was the captain of the *Titanic*. The ship hit an iceberg. Survivors saw Smith walking on the ship before it sank. William Lewis Herndon was the captain of the *Central America*. A storm damaged the ship. Two ships came to the rescue. They could only save some people. Herndon stayed behind. He let others get saved. Takeo Hirose was captain of the *Fukui Maru*. A Russian ship hit his ship. Hirose looked for survivors. He sank with the ship. These captains were brave.

Chase sailed on several ships. He finally became a captain. He sailed for 19 years. He went home for a short time every two or three years. He had children. He married four times.

Chase stored food in his attic. He was afraid of starving again. He had bad headaches. He was sent to a special home. He was declared **insane**. Insane means crazy. Chase couldn't forget what happened. And neither can we. This is a survival story for all time.

Some whaling trips could take 5 years.

Did You Know?

- Herman Melville wrote *Moby Dick*. The characters in the book represent real-life people. Ahab is Captain George Pollard. Starbuck is Owen Chase.

- Starbucks is a coffee company. It's named after Starbuck from *Moby Dick*.

- This was a popular cheer in Nantucket: "Death to the living. Long life to the killers. Success to sailors' wives. And greasy luck to whalers."

- Today's sperm whales are 65 feet (20 m) long. They used to be 100 feet (30.5 m) long. Scientists think whaling reduced the number of large male sperm whales. This caused them to be smaller.

- People saw omens before the *Essex* set sail. Omens are signs of bad luck. A comet crossed the skies. Locusts destroyed the crops. People saw a sea monster.

- Chase was going to harpoon the huge white whale. But the whale's tail was near the rudder. Rudders steer ships. If Chase hurt the whale, it might destroy the rudder. Chase didn't want to damage the rudder.

Consider This!

Take a Position: Read about whaling. Learn why some countries still hunt whales. Learn why some groups are against whaling. Should whaling be banned? Argue your point with reasons and evidence.

Say What? Read a version of Herman Melville's *Moby Dick*. Or watch a movie version. Compare the book to the true story of the *Essex*. Explain how they're the same. Explain how they're different.

Think About It! Whaling decreased the number of sperm whales. There used to be 1.6 million whales. Today, there are fewer than 360,000 whales. How else have humans affected other animals? Have humans been good or bad for nature? How so?

Learn More

- Cook, Peter, and David Antram, illust. *You Wouldn't Want to Sail on a 19th-Century Whaling Ship! Grisly Tasks You'd Rather Not Do*. New York: Franklin Watts, 2004.

- Currie, Stephen. *Thar She Blows: American Whaling in the Nineteenth Century*. Minneapolis: Lerner Publishing, 2001.

- Philbrick, Nathaniel. *Revenge of the Whale: The True Story of the Whaleship Essex*. New York: G. P. Putnam, 2002.

Glossary

cannibals (KAN-uh-buhlz) people who eat other people

crew (KROO) workers

harpoons (hahr-POONZ) long spears attached to ropes

insane (in-SANE) crazy

Jonah (JOH-nuh) unlucky sailor

lances (LANS-iz) long, sharp knives on poles

listed (LIST-id) tilted

mate (MAYT) an officer on a ship, lower than a captain

masts (MASTS) long poles on ships that carry sails

mess mates (MES MATES) sailor friends

pod (PAHD) family or group of whales

stove (STOHV) hit

stranded (STRAND-id) abandoned or stuck, left in danger

whaler (WAY-lur) special ship designed to catch whales

whaling (WALE-ing) the hunting of whales

Index

About the Author

Dr. Virginia Loh-Hagan is an author, university professor, former classroom teacher, and curriculum designer. She saw a play about the *Essex* with her book club. She lives in San Diego with her very tall husband and very naughty dogs. To learn more about her, visit www.virginialoh.com.